MURRAY WALKER'S

FORMULA ONE HEROES

Dear Reader,

As this updated edition of my book is published in October 2001, I will – with deep regret – just have done my last Formula One television commentary. Fifty-three years – for that is what it has been – is a long time for anything, but for commentating on one sport it is a very long time!

When I reported to my BBC Radio producer for the British Grand Prix at Silverstone in 1949 (no TV coverage in those days), Stirling Moss was a boy and the cars I was going to be talking about had their engines at the front. The drivers wore short-sleeved T-shirts, linen trousers and fabric skull-caps. They had no safety belts, the cars were mobile death traps that were – in effect – high-powered petrol tanks with absolutely no crash protection, and the massive crowd was separated from the projectiles on the track by a piece of rope. There were no barriers, no gravel traps and the medical facilities were minimal.

Things are very different now, with safety improved beyond recognition, all the slick sophistication of pit-stops, digital timing, luxurious motor homes, fast-moving and high-stepping promotion, electronics everywhere, superb presentation and, thanks to the miracle of television, the ability to watch the racing, live and in real time, from anywhere in the world. It has been my enormous privilege to see it all happen, to work with some wonderful people, watch and talk about motor racing's greats and marvel at their cars. I am going to miss it more than I can say.

But time waits for no man, and it certainly isn't going to wait for me. We all deteriorate and I am no exception, which is why I have always been determined to stop while I am still ahead with the viewers, rather than hang on until they think I'm past it. I just have a gut feeling that now is the time to wind down. So farewell but not goodbye and, from the bottom of my heart, my thanks and gratitude to all the wonderful people in motor sport who have made my life such a joy, particularly the fans on the other side of the track whose enthusiasm and friendship have supported me over the years.

Read on and you'll see who my Heroes have been, but the beauty of this truly great sport is that, as it develops, there will be plenty more to come!

This edition published in 2001 by
Virgin Books Ltd
Thames Wharf Studios
Rainville Road
London W6 9HA

First published in 2000 by Virgin Publishing

This edition produced for
The Book People Ltd,
Hall Wood Avenue, Haydock,
St Helens WA11 9UL

ISBN 1 85227 032 2

Art direction and design by Derek Slatter and
Katherine Spokes at Slatter-Anderson.

Printed and bound in Italy.

MURRAY WALKER'S

FORMULA ONE HEROES

MURRAY WALKER
& SIMON TAYLOR

TED SMART

CONTENTS

I guess it is true to say that my addiction to motor sport is an inherited genes thing. For would I have had this passion if I'd been the son of a plumber? Who knows, but I doubt it.

My beloved father, Graham Walker, was a kind, generous, cheerful and friendly man with a wonderful way with words and a personality the size of a house. In World War One he was a despatch rider. Thereafter he made a very healthy living racing motorcycles for some 15 years, and was a truly great competitor. Riding for Norton, Sunbeam and Rudge-Whitworth - all now sadly just memories from Britain's great two-wheeled racing past - he won the Isle of Man TT when it mattered more than all the other top races put together. He was the first home in many international Grands Prix, captained the winning British team in the prestigious International Six Days Trial (in which I was, much later, proudly to win a Gold Medal myself), and was one of the greatest motorcycling all-rounders the world has ever seen.

All this was happening from the time I was born in 1923 until only a few years before I left school. So, growing up in my famous father's shadow, I was likely either to love or to loathe motor sport. Actually, I was fairly unaffected by my unusual childhood because his dramatic occupation didn't strike me as being anything out of the ordinary. It was just what he did.

But the bug had bitten. All those idyllic holidays in the Isle of Man, Ulster, Holland, Belgium, Austria, Germany, Spain and France

Above: Nine-year-old Murray Walker stands proudly beside his father Graham, who has just finished second in the 1932 Isle of Man Lightweight TT on his 250cc Rudge-Whitworth.

Far right: Before my last British Grand Prix commentary for BBC TV in 1996, Bernie Ecclestone invited me to join Williams team-mates Jacques Villeneuve and Damon Hill in the drivers' pre-race parade in a Rolls-Royce Silver Ghost. Jacques won the race, but I already had the flowers!

watching my Dad winning races and being the hero of the crowds had their effect. When World War Two ended I left the army and took up motorcycle racing myself, in the fond belief that I'd show the Old Man how it should really be done.

Wrong! I wasn't nearly good enough, and anyway I was preoccupied with trying to build a successful career in the advertising business. So, after winning a heat at Brands Hatch (then an anti-clockwise *grass* track) on a 250cc AJS, I gracefully retired at the top of my inadequate form to comply with the old adage, "Those that can, do. Those that can't, talk about it!"

Again I was following in my father's footsteps, for when he left the saddle he became a great broadcaster whose radio commentaries from the TT course that he knew so well were the stuff of legend. For the 14 years until his death in 1962 we were the BBC's motorcycle commentary team and, in time, that led to my becoming its Formula One man.

But not for quite a while. Until 1978 I was primarily a bike chap who was also a gigantic car racing enthusiast. Motorcycle road races, trials and scrambles, I did them all, on radio and TV for the BBC, and on TV for ITV. Gradually I got into the car scene as well by way of rallycross, Formula Ford, Formula 3 and Touring Cars, with the occasional Formula One event to whet my appetite: like the 1969 German Grand Prix at the stunning original Nürburgring, when Jacky Ickx took his Brabham to victory, and the Ring again in 1974 for Clay Regazzoni's memorable Ferrari win.

And then in 1978 Jonathan Martin, BBC TV's Head of Sport, sent for me and said: "Murray, we're now going to do all the Formula One rounds, and I want you to handle the

Above: The start of my first-ever commentary for BBC Radio, the 1949 British Grand Prix at Silverstone. On the five-car front row are, from left, Villoresi and Bira (Maseratis), Walker (ERA), winner de Graffenried (Maserati) and Gerard (ERA).

commentary." Yes sir! Yes indeed!

Fifty-two years have now passed since my first-ever BBC commentary on the 1949 British Grand Prix at Silverstone, and 23 years since I was lucky enough to become TV's Formula One commentator. I can look back on a wonderfully happy life which has taken me round the world umpteen times as an enthusiastic and excited observer of the sport I love so much.

Motorcycles? Those immortals Jimmy Guthrie, Tim Hunt, Stanley Woods, Jimmy Simpson and Wal Handley were family friends, and my childhood "uncles" when we all stayed at the Castle Mona Hotel in Douglas for the Isle of Man TT races which, for me, still have a magic beyond words. Geoff Duke, Mike Hailwood, Phil Read, Giacomo Agostini, Jim Redman, John Surtees, Barry Sheene, Wayne Gardner and the other later greats were a lot more to me than just the people I revered and respected as some of the

greatest of all time. They were my friends.

Luck plays a major part in everybody's life, and I was privileged to be associated in a small way with Germany's world-beating Mercedes-Benz and Auto-Union teams when they came to England in 1937 and 1938 for the Donington Grands Prix. So I can put my hand on my heart and say, with truth, that I've stood beside Tazio Nuvolari, Bernd Rosemeyer, Rudolf Caracciola, Hermann Lang and the autocratic Manfred von Brauchitsch, and marvelled at their spectacular driving of the dominant, brutal silver-coloured high-tech monsters.

And since 1949, by virtue of my broadcasting life, I've been fortunate enough to have been where it's at as worldwide motor sport developed from its modest post-war beginnings to its current worldwide eminence. Do I appreciate my luck? I most certainly do, and I never cease to marvel at it. I've been massively privileged to meet and know so many great people, not just the drivers and riders but the officials, industry leaders and workers, the engineers, mechanics, sponsors, media people, enthusiasts and countless others who make motor sport so exciting and absorbing.

Time, then, to share my thoughts. Who were my true heroes? The drivers, the personalities and the folk behind the scenes: who were the people who have made the sport what it is? All will be revealed, but I must emphasise that they are *my* heroes, and also that I have not attempted to rank them in any order of absolute merit. That would have to be a very subjective affair when you're covering a period of over half a century.

Your own personal "Greats" may well be very different to mine. Was Fangio "greater" than Senna? Clark "greater" than Schumacher? Ascari "greater" than Prost? Each raced at different times to very different regulations, in very different cars, in very different circumstances and on very different circuits.

So I've chickened out. I have my views, of course. For me the fire, the style, the charisma, the all-round brilliance and the sheer ability to win races against overwhelming odds puts Tazio Nuvolari above all others, in the same way and for the same reasons that my friend the late Mike Hailwood is my all-time Number One motorcycle hero. But I can't prove it. It's not a mathematical or logical thing. It's a gut feeling based on my personal preferences and bias. I've simply

wandered down memory lane decade by decade, recalling the men and their feats who have meant the most to me. And I've slipped in a trio of circuits where my commentating adrenaline has flowed most freely. Not that it takes much to get it going anywhere!

I've cheated a bit, too. I've called this book *Murray Walker's Formula One Heroes*, so I'd better come clean about the fact that three of my heroes - Nuvolari, Caracciola and Rosemeyer - were pre-war aces and therefore never raced in the Formula

One World Championship. They're in simply because, Formula One or not, they're my heroes, and I couldn't bear to leave them out. So should I have included the great Christian Lautenschlager, who brilliantly won both the 1914 and 1918 French Grands Prix for Mercedes-Benz, and who was just as much a top man of his era as my heroes were of theirs? Maybe: but that would, I think, be going a step too far!

So read on and, agree or not, I hope you enjoy what's turned me on for all these years, and will continue to do so until I clamber into that great commentary box in the sky.

Above: Caracciola at speed in the 1938 Grand Prix Mercedes-Benz, the four-cam V12 W154, built to the new 3-litre formula. With this car he won the Swiss Grand Prix and the Coppa Acerbo at Pescara.

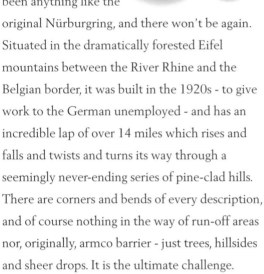

The concept of a worldwide international top class of racing - Formula One - was only dreamed up by the FIA in 1947, and until 1950 there was no World Championship. But there had been great motor sport for more than half a century before that. The first major races around the turn of the century were incredible city-to-city affairs across Europe, danger-laden battles through the dust in immense, crude Edwardian racers. The French ran the first Grand Prix in 1906, and the 1914 French GP, with its titanic struggle between Georges Boillot's Peugeot and Christian Lautenschlager's Mercedes, was one of the greatest races of all time.

But for the young and impressionable Murray Walker, the 1930s was a decade of unparalleled glamour and motor racing magic. For they were the legendary times of Tazio Nuvolari, Rudolf Caracciola and Bernd Rosemeyer, and of

Above: The tiny yellow-jerseyed figure of the Flying Mantuan is dwarfed in the big Auto Union's cockpit: Nuvolari on his way to victory in the 1938 Donington Grand Prix.

the fabled circuit where they had some of their finest victories: the Nürburgring. It was a long time before Formula One, but it was a halcyon period, and I feel privileged to have seen these historic superstars at work, and to have known

the Ring at its best.

There's never been anything like the original Nürburgring, and there won't be again. Situated in the dramatically forested Eifel mountains between the River Rhine and the Belgian border, it was built in the 1920s - to give work to the German unemployed - and has an incredible lap of over 14 miles which rises and falls and twists and turns its way through a seemingly never-ending series of pine-clad hills. There are corners and bends of every description, and of course nothing in the way of run-off areas nor, originally, armco barrier - just trees, hillsides and sheer drops. It is the ultimate challenge.

And here I have to declare a special interest, for my father Graham Walker won the first-ever motorcycle Grand Prix at the Nürburgring in 1927 - it lasted for over five and a half hours! - and then won it again in 1930. I still have the two magnificent gold rings that were part of his prize. Sadly, use of the full circuit was discontinued for Grands Prix for safety reasons after Niki Lauda was nearly killed there in 1976, but lesser events are still held on the old Ring, and for a small fee you can drive round in your road car.

To win at the Ring you had to be special, and it's no coincidence that my three pre-war heroes all turned in towering drives around that daunting and unfriendly track. None more so than the man I've already named my all-time racing hero, Tazio Nuvolari.

He was born in 1892 in a village not far from the northern Italian town of Mantua, and throughout his career he was known as *Il Mantovano Volante* - the Flying Mantuan. "Charisma" is a pretty hackneyed word these days, but no-one has ever had more than the fiery Nuvolari. Short, dark and wiry, he had a unique driving style, all energy, aggression and determined forcefulness, flinging his car into lurid four-wheel drifts, making non-stop steering corrections and literally willing it on to victory - even to the extent of beating his fist on the side of the cockpit to urge it on. In a red leather skull cap, blue cotton trousers and his traditional yellow pullover with a leather waistcoat on top, he was as colourful as his driving style, and one of the most versatile and successful drivers of all time.

Tazio was small and fearless, and the first of a lifetime of broken bones came from falling off a horse as a small boy. World War One delayed his start in motor sport, and he was in his late twenties when he began racing motorcycles. His

Above: The all-conquering 1932 Alfa Romeo team was run under the banner of Scuderia Ferrari. Drivers Baconin Borzacchini and Tazio Nuvolari flank a rarely smiling Enzo Ferrari.

Alberto
ASCARI

1950-1955 IN HIS FATHER'S WHEELTRACKS

From the Belgian Grand Prix in June 1952 to the Belgian Grand Prix in June 1953, every single World Championship round was won by the same man in the same type of car. It was a period of domination by one driver never seen before or since - in a modern context, almost like Michael Schumacher winning 18 races on the trot. The car was the fast, sturdy four-cylinder Ferrari 500, and the man was Alberto Ascari.

In many ways Italy is the country at the historical heart of motor racing. So it comes as a shock to realise that, while Michele Alboreto (1985) and Riccardo Patrese (1992) have filled the runner-up spot, and Castellotti, Musso and De Angelis all managed third in the table, no Italian has been World Champion since Ascari's two titles in 1952 and 1953. In fact, it was this plump, dapper man from Milan who was really responsible in the first place for building Ferrari's towering and enduring reputation as the most magical of all Formula One names.

Ascari came to epitomise the strength of Italy in motor sport, with his warm personality, his blue short-sleeved shirt and cotton trousers, and his trademark blue pudding-basin crash helmet. In fact, at a time when Britain dominated the two-wheeled racing world with Norton, AJS and Velocette, so Italy did the same in the four-wheeled world with Ferrari, Maserati and Alfa-Romeo, and Alberto Ascari stood as a symbol of that domination.

He was the son of one of the great Italian motor-racing heroes of the 1920s, Antonio Ascari. Now, I know what it's like to have a famous motor-sporting father, but I can't imagine what the effect must have been on the seven-year-old Alberto when his father was killed, leading the 1925 French Grand Prix in the rain. Perhaps Jacques Villeneuve may know. But one can speculate that it was the memory of his father that drove on Alberto Ascari to be the most successful driver of his day.

His strategy was always to win from the front, and in seven of his 13 Grand Prix victories he led from start to finish. At races he was cheerful and relaxed, and never seemed to be affected by pressure - although some said that he was not at his best when he had to fight through from behind. His chunky build belied his fitness and great stamina: as with Fangio, this showed in the heat of the annual Argentine round, and in 1953, in intense heat, he started from pole, led as usual from start to finish, set fastest lap, and lapped the entire field including his own Ferrari team-mates.

I never met Ascari, but I watched him race the red Ferraris at Silverstone in 1951, 1952 and 1953. That 1951 British Grand Prix was a turning

Right: Alberto Ascari with the spoils of yet another victory, at Silverstone in 1953. He scored his 13 Grand Prix wins in the space of 16 races.

Stirling *MOSS*

1952-1962 THE FIRST TRUE PROFESSIONAL

If I hadn't been me, I'd have liked to have been Stirling Moss! He is of my time and he's my countryman, and as far as I'm concerned he's not only the greatest British racing driver ever. He's also the most versatile racing driver of all time.

But more than that, he's a patriot, an honest man and a true sportsman. Hale, hearty and hugely energetic in his seventies, he's still racing and rallying the sort of cars he made famous when they were new. When you remember how many other British drivers of his era died young - Hawthorn, Collins, Bristow, Stacey, Scott-Brown, Wharton, Bueb, Lewis-Evans and too many more - it's our great good fortune that he's still with us.

And he so nearly wasn't. On Easter Monday 1962 he had that dreadful accident at Goodwood that put him in a coma for weeks, and almost killed him. It ended his professional racing career. But it's extraordinary to think that, even though he hasn't been a Formula One driver for almost 40 years, his name is still a household word. Even now, in the 21st century, if you carve up a London taxi and incur the wrath of the cabbie it'll be, not Nigel Mansell, not Damon Hill, but: "Who d'you think you are? Stirling Moss?"

Yet, for today's enthusiasts, Stirling Moss has been part of the scene for so long that I don't think many of them realise what a giant superstar he was. At a time when motor racing was not of major national interest, his every move on and off the track was front-page news. Every schoolboy knows he is the greatest driver never to have won the World Championship - he finished second four years running - but few know that he took part in an incredible 496 races. He finished in 366,

and of those, even more incredibly, he won 222, which is over 60 per cent.

More than 50 of his wins were in Formula One - there were a lot of non-championship F1 races back then - but Stirling would race anything and everything: sports cars, GTs, touring cars, F2, F3 and *formule libre*. At the big meetings he'd turn out in five or six races, in different cars. One measure of his prolific success is the BRDC Gold Star, effectively an all-formula World Championship awarded on points across all classes of international racing. Stirling won it ten times. He even found time to try rallying, and became one of the few people ever to win a Coupe d'Or for completing the gruelling Alpine Rally three years running without losing a single point.

And, wherever he was in a race, whether fighting for the lead or way down the field, whatever the odds, he would always give it everything, dig deep, 110 per cent. That's why the crowds loved him. It's significant that when he had that Goodwood accident he'd lost many

Right: Stirling Moss with the spoils of yet another victory, after winning the Grand Prix-length Silver City Trophy at Brands Hatch in 1961, his last full season.

Jackie STEWART

1965-1973 THE FIRST MODERN F1 DRIVER

Many great drivers, if they've lived long enough to retire, become shadows when they stop racing. It's as though God meant them to be racers, and didn't equip them to do anything else. Their competitive spirit, and their lust for excitement and glamour, cannot find an outlet. They become bored and miserable.

None of that applies to Jackie Stewart. He drove his last race more than a quarter of a century ago, crowning nine years in Formula 1 with 27 victories and three World Championships. All that makes him one of the greatest of all time. Yet since he stopped racing he's been busier than ever. He's played a senior executive role in multi-national companies like Ford and Goodyear. He's become a successful TV commentator and personality, particularly in North America. As a basis for his son Paul's own motor-racing career, he set up a racing team that has achieved unparalleled success in Formula Three, and has put several drivers on the ladder to stardom - including another well-known Scot, David Coulthard. And then in 1995, at the age of 56, he announced that he was going to start his own Formula One team.

To get Stewart Grand Prix off the ground Jackie drew on his long relationship with Ford, and used his prodigious sales skills to attract large sums in sponsorship from blue-chip companies. No-one understood better than he did how tough it is to start up an F1 team, and how many before him had seen their big ideas founder in a sea of debt and disaster. But the very qualities that made Jackie an exceptional racing driver also made him an exceptional manager, and a lot of that rubbed off on his son Paul, who became managing director of Stewart Grand Prix while Jackie filled the role of chairman. His drive to succeed, and his ability to gather round him a strong and talented team, meant that the team not only survived: it became, before the end of its third season, a race winner.

Nowadays Formula One is a matter for huge corporations and billion-dollar budgets, which makes Jackie's achievement all the more astonishing. I believe the history books will show him to be the last individual, as opposed to a major company like Toyota, to have started up an F1 team from scratch. And, fully understanding that life in F1 could only become ever harder for the smaller teams, in 1999 he sold the whole enterprise - for a sum rumoured to be around £80 million - to the Ford Motor Co, who rebadged it as Jaguar.

All this was a long way from the small family garage in Dumbartonshire where the teenage Jackie, a failure at school thanks to undiagnosed dyslexia, served at the pumps. But the will to win was already there: in clay-pigeon shooting he

Above: A superb result in Stewart Grand Prix's first season was Rubens Barrichello's second place in the rain at Monaco.

"As soon as Jackie got into a single-seater for the first time, Ken Tyrrell could not believe how quick, and how smooth, he was."

Below: Stewart's sojourn at BRM started brilliantly, but ended with the difficult and unreliable H16. This jump at the Nürburgring in the 1967 German Grand Prix was all for naught: Jackie retired with transmission failure.

found something that he could excel in, and at the age of 16 he was shooting for Scotland. His elder brother Jimmy had been a sports car racer in the 1950s, and soon Jackie persuaded a wealthy customer of the garage to let him race his cars in local events. This led to drives for the national Scottish team Ecurie Ecosse, and his name came to the attention of Ken Tyrrell, who was then planning his Cooper Formula Three team for 1964.

What actually happened was this Scots lad went testing Ecurie Ecosse's elderly Cooper Monaco sports-racer at Goodwood, and the circuit manager, Robin McKay, was so astonished by his speed that he told his friend Ken Tyrrell all about it. Tyrrell phoned Dumbarton and invited the youngster back to Goodwood for a test. As soon as Jackie got into a single-seater for the first

time, Ken could not believe how quick, and how smooth, he was: here clearly was a natural ability which recalled that other Scot, Jim Clark. Ken hired him on the spot, and it was the start of a relationship between the young Scotsman and the tall, no-nonsense timber merchant that, in time, was to take both of them to the top of Formula One.

Jackie swept all before him in F3, winning every race except two (in one of which his clutch failed on the warm-up lap). Not surprisingly, this domination generated offers from no fewer than three F1 teams for the 1965 season. He plumped for BRM alongside Graham Hill, and the results came straight away: a point in his first Grand Prix (Kyalami), a podium in his second (Monte Carlo), second places in his third and fourth (Spa and Clermont Ferrand). At Monza he led his team-

mate over the line to score his first Grand Prix victory, and he finished third in his first World Championship season. It was an astonishing achievement.

The following year Stewart had an accident which was to have a major effect on him, and would indirectly exert a fundamental influence on the future of Formula One. The Belgian Grand Prix on the frighteningly fast old Spa track started in the dry, but it was raining on the far side of the circuit. Seven cars went off as they suddenly ran into the rain on that first lap. Jackie lost control on the notorious Masta Curve, a 150mph kink between two roadside cottages. Hill went off at the same place, scrambled from his BRM unhurt, and ran to the wreckage of his team-mate's car.

Jackie was trapped inside, semi-conscious, and soaked in fuel from a ruptured tank. By the time help arrived and he was removed from the remains of the car, he'd been trapped for almost half an hour. Had there been a fire, it would have been the end of him. In fact he recovered quickly, and was racing again five weeks later: but the crash taught him that many of F1's dangers were avoidable. That was when he vowed to make it his responsibility to improve racing safety.

BRM's great days were past and, though Jackie stayed with them for a third season, his only two finishes were a brave second at Spa, driving with one hand and holding the H16 in gear, and a third in the little V8 BRM on the

Bugatti circuit at Le Mans. However he was still driving for Ken Tyrrell in Formula Two, using a

French Matra chassis, and for 1968 Ken decided to take the plunge and move into Formula One, with a Cosworth DFV-powered Matra. Stewart had an offer from Ferrari, but as soon as he knew Uncle Ken was going into F1 there was no choice: he wanted to be in his team. And now, for wee Jackie, things really began to happen.

He won three Grands Prix that first year with Ken, at Zandvoort, the Nürburgring and Watkins Glen, and finished second in the World Championship. In fact he probably would have won the title, had he not broken his wrist in a Formula Two accident, which forced him to miss two Grands Prix and drive in several more with his wrist in a plastic support. The German victory that year was one of the greatest of his career. The challenging 14-mile circuit was cloaked with

Above: Jackie scored six wins out of 11 rounds in the 1971 championship in the Tyrrell 003, and had clinched his second title well before the end of the season.

Mario
ANDRETTI

1968-1982 THE AMERICAN DREAM

MURRAY'S NOTES

• *Incredible achiever: from humble immigrant beginnings to America's top driver before he even got to F1*

• *Charismatic figure who is still the best known racer in the USA, but approachable*

• *Victorious in every discipline he attempted, and still an enthusiast who hates to stop racing*

FACTS

Born: Montona, Italy, 28 February 1940
Grands Prix: 128
First Grand Prix: Watkins Glen 1968, Lotus
Last Grand Prix: Las Vegas 1982, Ferrari
Wins: 12
Pole positions: 18
Points: 180
Points per start: 1.41
Percentage of wins: 9%
World Champion: 1978, Lotus Ronnie Peterson

In the 1952 Italian Grand Prix, while the excited Monza crowd cheered on the Ferraris of Villoresi, Farina, Taruffi and their hero Ascari, a slight, shabby 12-year-old boy pressed up against the fence and marvelled at what he saw. When I become a man, he thought, this was what I will do. But he'd been born into war-time poverty, and had spent much of his childhood in a displaced persons' camp. The wire fence between him and the roaring red cars could not be more impenetrable. How could a poor kid with nothing ever realise his dream to be World Champion?

Yet fairy tales do come true - if they are helped along by iron will, ceaseless determination and unshakeable self-belief. Within 20 years that poor kid would drive, and win, for Ferrari. And within 30 he would be Champion of the World.

Anyone who starts where Mario Andretti started, and achieves what he has achieved, is a hero. Mario is a personification of the American Dream, because his family emigrated to the USA when he was 15, settling in the Pennsylvania town of Nazareth, where he lives still. As soon as they were old enough Mario and his twin brother Aldo started racing stock cars, midgets and sprint cars in local events. Aldo's career was blighted by a serious crash, but Mario went from strength to strength, learning hard lessons in the tough world of American speedway racing. By 1965 the young Italian immigrant was top dog, and over five seasons he was USAC Champion three times and runner-up twice, winning the Indianapolis 500 and, in NASCAR, the Daytona 500.

Back then no USAC driver had ever successfully transferred to Formula One. Few

had wanted to try. But Mario's childhood memories of Monza were deep-rooted. He'd met Colin Chapman and Jimmy Clark at Indianapolis, both of whom had been highly impressed with his ability. After Clark was killed in 1968 Colin persuaded Mario into a Lotus 49 for the American Grand Prix at Watkins Glen, and he made history by starting his first Formula One race from pole position.

From then on he did as much Formula One as his USAC commitments would allow, and in 1970 his American sponsors, STP, ran a March for him in five Grands Prix. This was not the competitive car he'd hoped for, and it brought him only one podium, in Spain. But in 1971 he realised the next stage of his dream by signing for Ferrari. His first race for the Scuderia was the South African Grand Prix at Kyalami - and the fairy tale continued, because he won it.

But that was to be his last Grand Prix victory for almost five years, although success continued to come in USAC, sports cars and Formula A. He spent a couple of fruitless F1 seasons with the

Above: In the superb ground-effects Lotus 79 Cosworth, Mario Andretti leads his 1978 season-long shadow, team-mate Ronnie Peterson. Andretti took eight pole positions and won six times to become America's second World Champion.

Niki LAUDA

1971-1985 HIS OWN MAN

A key ingredient in the make-up of a great racing driver is determination: determination to achieve the goals you set yourself, determination to conquer all set-backs. If there's one man who has had to demonstrate that quality more than anyone else in the history of motor sport, it's Niki Lauda.

Niki was never a conformist. After no great early success in F3 and sports cars, he took out a bank loan to fund a Formula Two season in 1971, and then struggled as a pay driver at the lower end of the F1 grids in 1972 for March, where he was very much in Peterson's shadow, and in 1973 for BRM. But even in the uncompetitive BRM there were flashes of brilliance - like running third at Monaco before the gearbox went - and for 1974 he was invited to join Ferrari alongside the far more experienced Clay Regazzoni.

Ferrari had been without a win for more than a year, but Lauda's determination came to the fore with a relentless schedule of development testing which was beneficial to both car and driver. He was second in his first race for the Scuderia in Argentina, and went on to score wins in Spain and Holland, but there was a string of retirements too. His team-mate Clay Regazzoni was more consistent, and ended up second in the championship, while Niki was only fourth. For 1975 the determined Austrian vowed to do better.

And he did, with a tremendous five-race run from Monaco to France that produced four wins and a second, and assured him of the World Championship - the first for a Ferrari driver since John Surtees more than a decade before. Lauda was set fair to win the 1976 title, too, in a dramatic season-long battle with James Hunt -

with whom he was very friendly off the track: two non-conformists together. He took four wins and two seconds in the first six races, but then, on the old Nürburgring, came the dreadful accident that should have taken his life.

On the second lap his Ferrari suddenly lurched to the right and into the barriers on a fast part of the track, presumably because of some mechanical breakage, and bounced back into the path of Brett Lunger's Surtees. The Surtees hit the Ferrari amidships and pushed it, now on fire, down the track, with the unconscious Lauda still inside. There were no marshals or medical teams nearby, and no safety car in those days, so it was left to other drivers who'd stopped - Guy Edwards, Arturo Merzario, Lunger, Harald Ertl - to wade into the flames and save his life.

Horribly burned, he lay close to death for several days: yet, unbelievably, he turned up at Monza six weeks later, with the burns to his head, face, lungs and upper body far from healed, and insisted on starting the race. His fourth place that day was one of the bravest drives in Formula One's 50-year history.

Right: Single-minded, uncompromising and non-conformist, Niki Lauda is truly a very unusual human being.

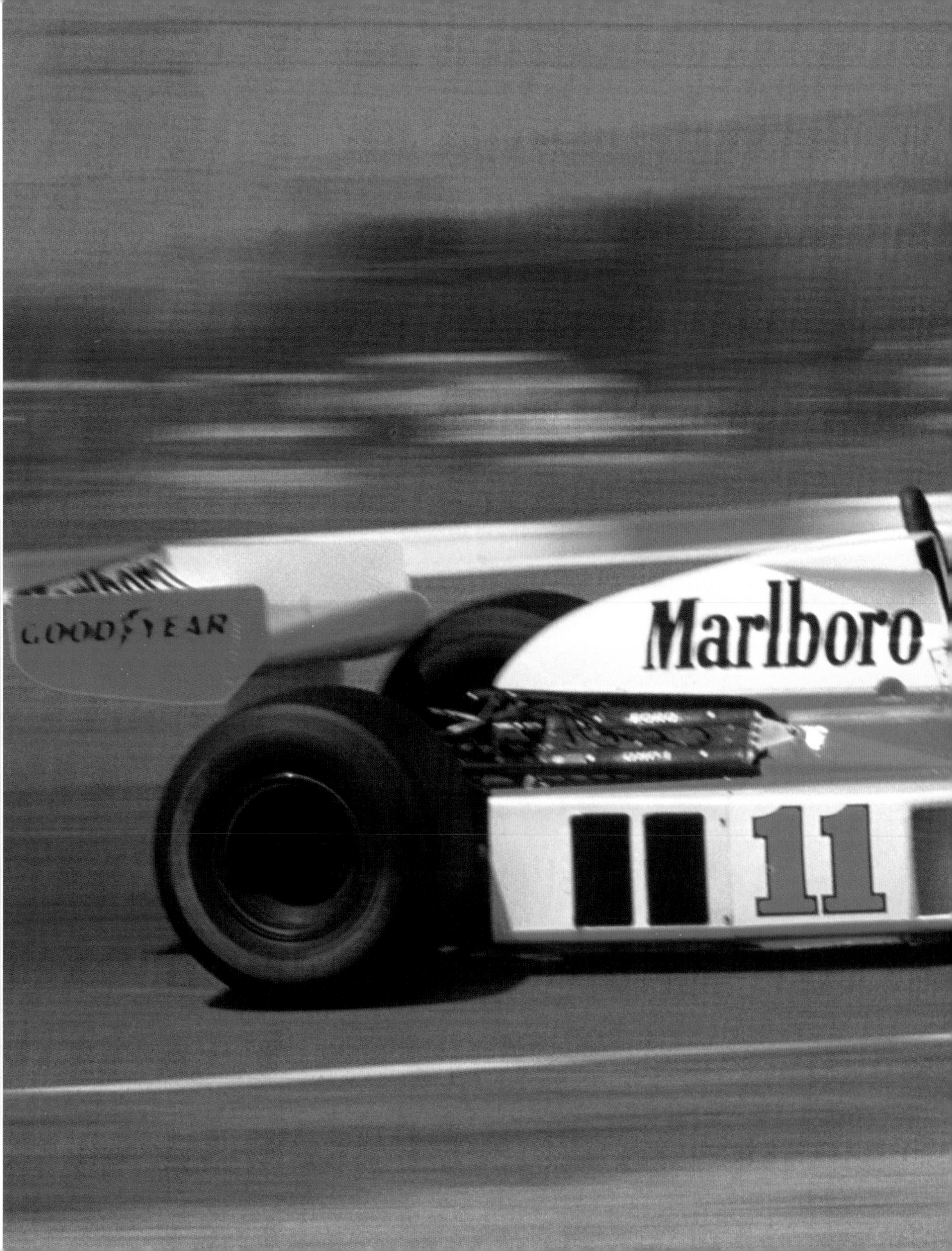
GOODYEAR
Marlboro
11

Alan
JONES

MURRAY'S NOTES

- *Gruff, rough, tough and outspoken*

- *Doggedly trod stony path from Australia via Earl's Court to a world title*

- *Was in the right place at the right time in his relationship with the Williams team: they suited each other perfectly, and drew the best from each other*

FACTS

Born: Melbourne, Australia,
2 November 1946
Grands Prix: 116
First Grand Prix: Montjuich
1975, Stiller Hesketh
Last Grand Prix: Adelaide
1986, Haas Lola
Wins: 12
Pole positions: 6
Points: 206
Points per start: 1.77
Percentage wins: 10%
**World champion: 1980,
Williams**

Sporting heroes often display their national characteristics to extremes. Think of most people's concept of the Australian male, and you come up with words like tough, uncompromising, humorous, plain-speaking, determined and sheer bloody-minded. With each of those adjectives, you could be describing Alan Jones.

Some like Alan, some loathe him. I'm very much in the former category, and for me it's those same rough tough qualities that make him one of the modern heroes of F1. I knew him well throughout his racing career, and have worked with him many times since, in the commentary box at the Australian Grand Prix. He's very refreshing - direct, tells it like it is, and certainly doesn't mince his words. Which is just how he always was as a World Champion. In the F1 paddocks, the more feathers he ruffled, the happier he was.

Alan comes from a motor-racing family. His father Stan Jones was a tough guy too. He raced a Maserati 250F and the ferocious locally-brewed Maybach Special, and won the Australian and New Zealand Grands Prix. On his day he beat Jack Brabham, and he died still regretting that he'd never tried his luck on the world stage by pulling up his roots and coming to Europe. He was a car dealer, and while Alan was growing up he was doing very well. Alan by his own admission was a spoilt kid who got pretty much whatever he wanted, including karts to race - he was a class champion at 15 - and an MG for his 16th birthday. As soon as he was old enough he was racing his dad's Cooper-Climax, and winning in that too.

Then Stan's business went bust, and suddenly

Alan found out about the harder side of life. But he followed his dream and came to England, with £50 in his pocket. He found a room in a basement flat in Earl's Court and started dealing in cars by the roadside, selling old vans to Australian tourists, living hand to mouth and saving every penny. In a year he'd got enough cash to buy an old Formula Ford and go racing, but that was written off in a test session by a friend. More vans got sold, and Alan managed to buy an old F3 Lotus. This was written off in a test session, too, breaking Alan's leg. But Alan was made of determined stuff. He found another car and stuck it out in Formula Three, eventually getting enough backing to run in Formula Atlantic and then Formula 5000. He had his good races, he had his bad races, but all the while the hand-to-mouth existence of the impoverished British racer was blending with his inbred Aussie toughness to build a case-hardened character.

His break into F1 came in 1975 in a privately-entered Hesketh run by former F3 driver Harry Stiller. In four races he had two accidents and a wheel fall off, and then in the fourth he finished

Right: A familiar 1980 sight! Alan triumphantly raises his winner's trophy after the USA East GP at Watkins Glen.

Nigel
MANSELL

1980-1995 TRUE GRIT

MURRAY'S NOTES

• *The nation's hero: worshipped by the British fans like no-one before or since, and loved to play to the crowd*

• *Lion-hearted in the cockpit, persecution complex out of it*

• *A driver with unshakeable determination, a huge will to win, and above all immense on-track ability, which his many critics frequently forget. Brilliant achievements in Indycar racing also*

FACTS

Born: Upton-on-Severn, England, 8 August 1953
Grands Prix: 187
First Grand Prix: Zeltweg 1980, Lotus
Last Grand Prix: Barcelona 1995, McLaren
Wins: 31
Pole positions: 32
Points: 482
Points per start: 2.6
Percentage wins: 17%
World Champion: 1992, Williams

Silverstone, 1977. "Come with me", said ace talent-spotter John Thornburn. "I want you to meet someone who's going to the top." I went, because John knows what he's about. The man I was introduced to was a 24-year-old, in his second season of Formula Ford, called Nigel Mansell. "Pleasant chap", I thought. "He's a Brummie from Hall Green, like me." I was to see a lot more of him over the next 18 years.

Nigel had come from an impressive apprenticeship in karts and, despite breaking his neck, he did well in Formula Ford - well enough to fight his way into Formula Three. It has become legend that he quit his job, sold his house to pay for a March F3 drive, relied on his loyal and charming wife Rosanne to be the breadwinner, and caught the eye of no less a person than Colin Chapman. It was after damaging his spine that the call came to test for the Lotus Formula One team. Nigel stuffed himself full of pain killers, and got the drive.

The years of sacrifice and denial were to prove a great investment. Nigel went on to become statistically Britain's most successful racing driver, with 31 victories and 482 points out of 187 Grand Prix starts. He was World Champion in 1992, spent two seasons with Ferrari - every racing driver's dream - and added to all that the unique achievement of winning America's demanding Indy Championship in his first year.

Nigel is an extraordinary mixture. In the cockpit he was inspired: gutsy, single-mindedly determined, awesomely brave and with an implacable will to win. He gave me more magic commentary moments than all the rest of them put together, because wherever he was there was drama and excitement. Collapsing in the searing heat of Dallas as he tried to push his broken Lotus to the finish. Passing Senna's McLaren in his Ferrari to win in Hungary. Unbelievably taking Gerhard Berger on the outside of Mexico's notorious Peraltada. Losing a wheel in the pitlane in Portugal. Jinking past Nelson Piquet at Stowe to win the 1987 British Grand Prix. Grimly paralleling Senna in Spain, wheel-to-wheel with sparks flying at 200 mph, until Ayrton backed off. Losing the 1986 World Championship in Adelaide when a tyre blew at 190 mph. Taking a sensational second place at a sodden 1988 Silverstone in a car that truly wasn't capable of it. The last laps of Monaco in 1992 when he all but drove over the top of Senna's McLaren in his fruitless bid to win. His dramatic departure from Williams. The physical confrontation with Senna in Belgium. Black-flagged in Portugal for reversing in the pitlane. The list just goes on and excitingly on.

Not only that: Nigel was a brilliant showman. He has always seen himself as a man of the

Right: "He loves them and they love him," I shouted into the microphone ecstatically and it was true. Nigel warmed to the adulation he received for his gutsy driving and returned it on the podium, in the pitlane and wherever he met his adoring public.

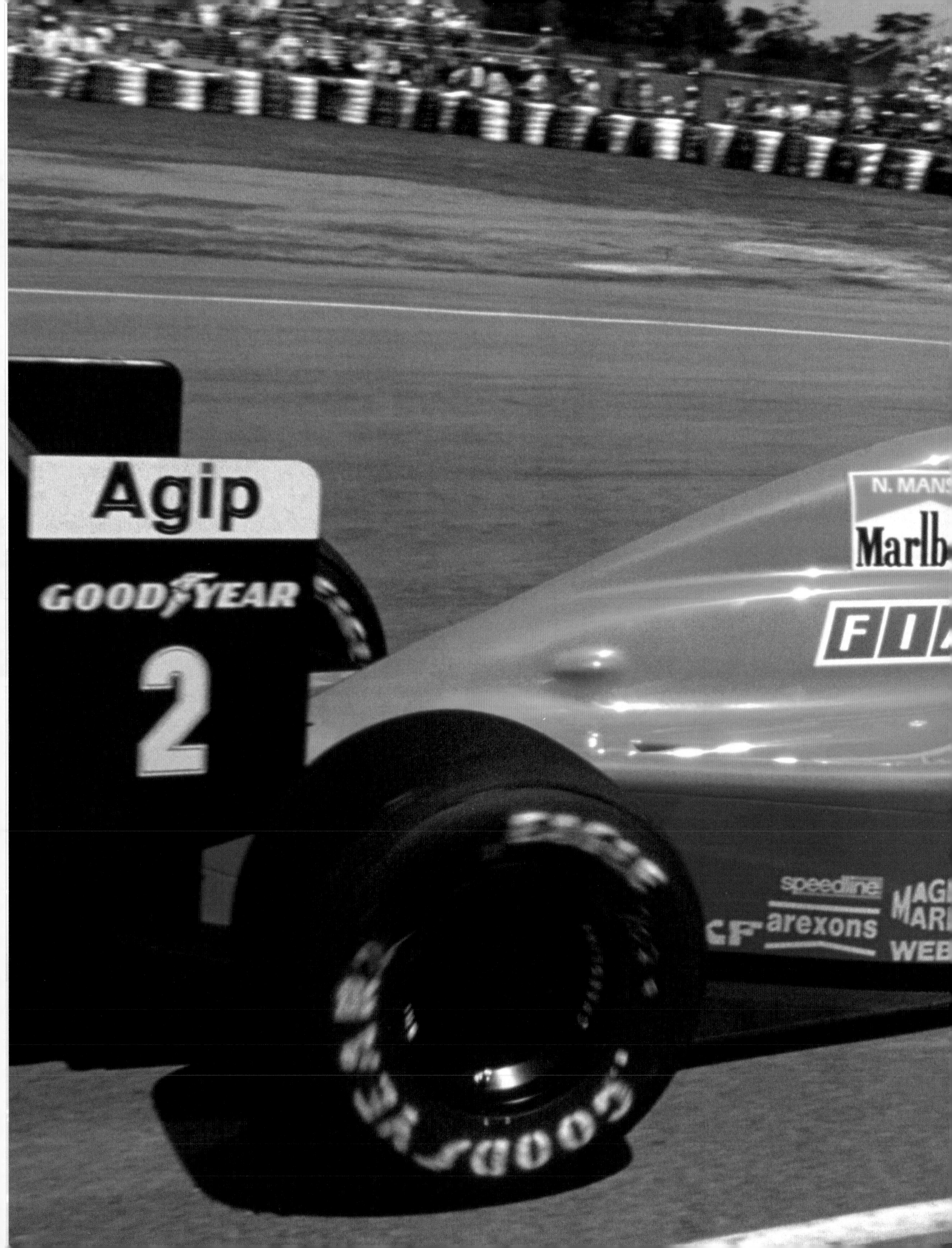
Agip
GOODYEAR
2
speedline
arexons

Alain
PROST

1980-1993 THE PROFESSOR

If greatness were just a matter of statistics, Alain Prost would stand head and shoulders above the rest. He raced in Formula One for 13 seasons, and won 51 Grands Prix - more than a quarter of the 199 he started, and a total no other driver has approached. He was World Champion four times, more than anyone else except Fangio, and racked up an unbeaten total of 798.5 points. That's an average of four points every race - like finishing on the podium every single time! - and during that golden period he had to race against the likes of Lauda, Piquet, Mansell, Senna and Schumacher to do it.

But there's more to being a Formula One Hero than mere statistics. Alain Prost was a perfectionist, a man who approached every part of the job of going motor racing with care and deep thought. Not for nothing was his nickname The Professor. He was always hugely quick, but he was never the most spectacular driver to watch. Smooth, disciplined and controlled, he tended not to be the driver whose exploits you talked about at the airport, waiting for the plane home after the race. But he'd usually beaten all the men you *were* talking about!

Prost had in spades the burning will to win and unshakeable motivation that drive all great champions. But in his case it was combined from the start with a quietly-spoken common sense, a strong awareness of what he believed was right and wrong, and a refusal to take risks for no purpose. For example, he was honest about his dislike of racing in the rain: he could be very quick on a wet track if he had to be, but he was prepared to stick by his principles and withdraw if he

thought conditions were needlessly dangerous - as he did in Australia in 1989.

Alain also possessed remarkable political and diplomatic skills, and was a past-master at gathering the entire personnel of a team around him - as Nigel Mansell found to his dismay when Prost joined him at Ferrari in 1990. He even out-manoeuvred the politically astute Ayrton Senna when both were vying for Mansell's seat at Williams in 1993. He was always adroit in his handling of the media, too. I must have interviewed him hundreds of times, and always he was patient, direct, courteous and good-humoured - all part of his professionalism and attention to detail.

Prost's early career followed the classic route: teenage success in karting leading to victory in the European Championship, then French and European titles in Formula Renault and Formula Three. He was already 25 when, in 1980, he made his F1 debut for McLaren, finishing in the points in his first two races. Then he moved to Renault for three seasons. The yellow cars weren't very reliable, but they were fast, and when Alain finished it was

Right: Prost's 28th Grand Prix victory put him ahead of Stewart in total wins, but he went on to hit a record-setting total of 51.

Martin
BRUNDLE

Martin Brundle is a very special bloke, as I have good reason to know. He may never have won a Grand Prix, but I regard that as being just as much an unjustified quirk of Formula One as the fact that Stirling Moss never won a World Championship. And he came near a few times. When Michael Schumacher retired from the 2000 Monaco Grand Prix, allowing his friend David Coulthard to score a magnificent win, Martin said with a rueful grin: "I wish Schuey's rear suspension had broken in 1994!" - because that was when Martin's McLaren finished second to Schumacher's Benetton around the punishing street circuit.

As I've already said, I've been lucky enough to have commentated for so long that men I knew, respected and liked as drivers have become my friends after they retired from racing. None more so than Martin, who never achieved the Formula One success that his talent deserved. It's probably fair to say that he only had one season when he was in the right team at the right time, which was Benetton in 1992. And that was when he had the misfortune to have Michael Schumacher as his team-mate.

I first got to know Martin in 1983, during one of the greatest seasons ever of the prestigious British Formula Three Championship, when he and Ayrton Senna battled for the title. In the early part of the season the Brazilian built up a big lead by sensationally winning the first nine rounds of the 20-race series, with Martin almost invariably second. But Martin never gave up believing he could beat Senna, and mid-season he started to do it. He scored six victories in the next nine

rounds. Twice they collided, on one occasion earning Senna a £200 fine and a licence endorsement, and once Senna went off on his own trying to pass Martin. It all came down to the final shoot-out at Thruxton: but that day Ayrton made no mistakes and Martin had to be content with second place.

Both drivers were obviously ripe for immediate promotion to Formula One. Senna was snapped up by Toleman and, in short order, went on to success with Lotus and glory with McLaren. But it was infinitely tougher for Martin. Nevertheless, he had a brilliant start in 1984 with the ever-underfunded Tyrrell team - fifth in his first race, in Brazil, and a magnificent second in his eighth outing in Detroit. He'd come through from 11th on the grid, and was beaten to the flag by World Champion Nelson Piquet by less than a second.

Then it all began to unravel. Two weeks after Detroit, his career suffered a major setback when he broke both ankles in a massive practice crash at the temporary Dallas track. And then all Tyrrell's results for the season were wiped away

Right: Eleven tough F1 seasons have turned Martin Brundle into the shrewdest of observers of the Grand Prix scene.

Damon
HILL

MURRAY'S NOTES

• *Hard worker with bottomless determination more than making up for any shortfall in sheer natural ability. Was lucky to be in the best car at the right time, but made excellent use of it*

• *A nice chap, but intense and brooding under pressure. Loved and supported by the British public as an underdog who became World Champion through sheer effort*

• *Reached his zenith with championship at Williams: his career never recovered from his contract there not being renewed*

FACTS

Born: London, England, 17 September 1960
Grands Prix: 116
First Grand Prix: Silverstone 1992, Brabham
Last Grand Prix: Suzuka 1999, Jordan
Wins: 22
Pole positions: 20
Points: 360
Points per start: 3.1
Percentage wins: 19%
World Champion: 1996, Williams

I've had some emotional moments in my years in Formula One, but none more so than the end of the 1996 Japanese Grand Prix at Suzuka. "I've got to stop now," I said, "because I've got a lump in my throat," as Damon Hill crossed the line to become World Champion. You see, I'd known and commentated on his illustrious twice-World Champion father Graham, I'd watched him from his debut as a promising motorcycle racer to his dramatic years in Formula One, and I'd come to regard him as a friend. So his success, at the end of what I knew had been a long and very hard road, was very special to me.

Being the son of a famous father can be a mixed blessing, and in Damon's case it was especially so as he struggled to progress, constantly being compared with his Dad. Graham was always seen not as a natural genius, like Jim Clark, but as someone with indomitable determination and a huge capacity for hard work. Damon was the same. At 14, emerging from childhood, his privileged life was shattered by Graham's tragic death in an air crash. Suddenly things were very hard for the Hill family. But where there's a will there's a way. Damon's passion was motorbikes (he's still a massive enthusiast) and in 1984, with hard-won experience from going it alone, he became 350cc Clubmans Champion at Brands Hatch.

Then, thanks to his mother Bette, he took a course at the Winfield Racing School in France, and did well. Being Graham's son was helpful now, as doors opened for him that might not have opened for others. Formula Ford led to Formula Three, and thence to Formula 3000.

There were wins, but no championships. "He's a grafter, just like his dad," people said, but he was a lot more than that, and he was to outshine Graham in Formula One.

Damon is an intense, industrious and awesomely determined chap. He is also a witty, modest Englishman and a fine and loving father, is sensitive, kind, decent, honest and courteous, and has a dry sense of humour. But he is no pushover. In an immensely competitive environment his F3000 achievements impressed Frank Williams enough to sign him as test driver for the Williams team in 1991. His skill, patient dedication and mechanical sympathy gained him respect, and in 1993 he got his reward. Mansell was out and Hill was in, as number two to Alain Prost.

In his very first year, against Prost, Senna, Schumacher and the rest, he took three superb victories in succession, but his second season was traumatic. Prost had retired, to be replaced by Ayrton Senna, but at Imola, in only the third race of the year, the great Brazilian crashed his Williams and died. Amidst the deepest gloom

Right: Damon Hill came late to Formula One, but dogged persistence made him the first World Champion son of a Champion father.

Michael
SCHUMACHER

FACTS

Born: Hürth-Hermühlheim, Germany, 3 January 1969
Grands Prix: 154
First Grand Prix: Spa 1991, Jordan
Wins: 50
Pole positions: 39
Points: 756 (78 points removed in 1997 by FIA World Council)
Points per start: 4.9
Percentage wins: 32.5%
World Champion: 1994, Benetton; 1995, Benetton; 2000, Ferrari
(to French GP 2001)

Not altogether by chance, I was standing in the Jordan garage at the 1991 Belgian Grand Prix when Michael Schumacher got into his car to qualify. Just like everyone else, I wanted to see how this young German first-timer was going to get on. "Driving for Mercedes-Benz he's been a real flyer in the sports car series, and they've given Eddie Jordan a bung to see if he can cut the mustard in Formula One" was the story that took me there, and I was about to witness the start of one of the greatest careers in the history of the sport.

Slim and upright, obviously mega-fit, calm, very businesslike, confident, and having already achieved some remarkable testing times at Silverstone, he certainly looked the part. And by the end of the day he was the hottest property at Spa. He was to start his very first Grand Prix seventh on the grid, at one of the most demanding circuits of them all, beaten only by Senna, Prost, Mansell, Berger, Alesi and Piquet. Here was a man who was going places!

He was a former karting star who'd done Formula Ford and F3 in his home country and shown a lot of talent. In 1990, when he was 21, Mercedes-Benz signed up Schumacher and two other youngsters, Heinz-Harald Frentzen and Karl Wendlinger, to drive in their sports car team. Simultaneously Schumacher continued with F3 but went farther afield, winning in Japan and Macau. His fourth-row grid position for his first Grand Prix - on one of the most daunting circuits on the Grand Prix calendar - was a sensation, although his inexperience with an F1 clutch saw him retire virtually on the line.

Benetton bosses Flavio Briatore and Tom Walkinshaw were obviously anxious to benefit from this young man's urge to get to the top as quickly as possible, for at the Italian Grand Prix a fortnight later, Monza was in a ferment over the news that they had signed Schumacher - to the fury of an incandescent Eddie Jordan, who had failed to bind this glittering new prospect to his team. And Schumacher finished in the points in each of his first three races for Benetton. In his first full season he was on the podium five times in the first ten races: and then, 12 months after his first F1 drive at Spa, he was back there to beat Nigel Mansell's Williams by over half a minute and win the Belgian Grand Prix.

He hasn't looked back since. Double World Champion for Benetton in 1994 and 1995, he went on to lead Ferrari out of the wilderness to the promised land, and make himself one of the highest paid sportsmen in the world. There was no need for him to take on the daunting task of reviving Ferrari's fortunes in 1996, for he could undoubtedly have found a seat in just about any

Right: One of Michael Schumacher's most pleasing habits is his show of unrestrained delight when he climbs on to the top step of the podium.

Jerez, with a one-point lead. Controversy again, for as Villeneuve audaciously dived inside him Michael turned in on the Williams. They collided, and Schumacher was out, while Villeneuve came home third and took the title. The FIA held an enquiry, and decided to expunge all the championship points Schumacher had earned that year - though they left the race results in place.

Michael was second to Mika Hakkinen and McLaren in 1998, adding six more Ferrari wins to his total, and in 1999, after he'd won Imola and Monaco, it began to look as though he would take the championship to Ferrari at last. Then came the crash on the first lap of the British Grand Prix that broke his leg and kept him away from six races. But his recovery was rapid and in his comeback race in Malaysia he was instantly dominant, before waving Eddie Irvine past to help his championship chances.

Despite his immense achievements, Michael Schumacher is far from universally popular in Britain. His image is of a cold, arrogant, autocratic man. But, having interviewed him countless times, it is an image with which I could not disagree more. It is true that like Nigel Mansell, another of his few peers, he is seldom far from controversy, for he speaks his mind, and has also been associated with some contentious regulation-bending moves both at Benetton and Ferrari. I'd hardly call him charismatic, as Fangio

and Senna were, but I've never found Michael to be anything other than courteous, cheerful, friendly, helpful, totally professional and, moreover, immensely authoritative and eloquent in what is to him a foreign language. What he says is going to happen usually does, and I find it refreshing that, when Michael talks in front of the camera, there's none of the bland and irritating corporate speak used by so many of his rivals. He tells it like it is (admittedly often with a psychological spin to suit his requirements!).

To me, Michael's sheer happiness and exuberance when he leaps on to the top step of the podium are immensely endearing. Watch him leap about and punch the air: it makes a sharp contrast to so many of his rivals, who sometimes look as though you've given them a fiver and taken back ten quid. We've all got faults, and so has he, but for my money he is without peer: the greatest racing driver of his era, and one of the very greatest of all time. Altogether a class act.

Above: Blasting out of the Imola pits in the 1999 San Marino GP on his way to his fifteenth win for Ferrari.

Far left: Schumacher leads the queue into Ste Devote in the 1999 Monaco Grand Prix. He won it for the fourth time.

"MICHAEL'S SHEER HAPPINESS AND EXUBERANCE WHEN HE LEAPS ON TO THE TOP STEP OF THE PODIUM ARE IMMENSELY ENDEARING."

Backroom boys & girls

THEY ALSO SERVE

Heroic places

THREE GREAT CIRCUITS

Epilogue

Writing a book is hard work, but this one has been a very real pleasure for me. I have always led a full and busy life, first in my advertising career with broadcasting as my hobby and then, after I had given up the job, full-time as a commentator with all the other things that go with it. I've never been much of a chap for looking back and mulling over the past. So, in order to produce the book you're holding now, I've had to remind myself of all the people I've known in the world of motor sport, all the places I've been and all the things I've seen. It's made me realise how very lucky I've been.

Not just because of the races, the travel and the multitude of wonderful memories which I hope to write more about one day. Most of all because of the wonderful people that have made my entire life such a joy. Forty-eight years with the BBC is a very long time, but I enjoyed them

I felt immensely flattered, and the time I have spent with them has been no less enjoyable: particularly as I have been part of a team that I can say with complete conviction produces the best Grand Prix coverage in the world.

Thanks to the vision, leadership and commercial brilliance of Bernie Ecclestone, Formula One has developed in my time from a specialised sport in a few European countries with very little following among the general public to a mammoth enterprise which commands worldwide excitement and interest. It has been a quite incredible experience to have been associated with it all, and I certainly hope to continue as long as people want to hear what I have got to say, and I am physically and mentally able to say it.

The friends I have made and worked with are too numerous to detail, but there is one that I want to single out: Simon Taylor. The Heroes in this book and the memories of them are mine, and so are a lot of the words, but the rest are a joint effort, and I couldn't have hoped to work with a

Right: Authors at work on location. Murray Walker and Simon Taylor compare notes in the pits.

immensely, and always felt proud and privileged to work with what I firmly believe to be the world's greatest broadcasting organisation. When ITV invited me to join their Formula One team

more cheerful, helpful, knowledgeable and enthusiastic colleague. We both hope you've enjoyed reading it as much as we've enjoyed putting it together!

pp. 4/5 Grand Prix gladiators listen with varying expressions of impatience and cynicism to the drivers' briefing on the grid before the 1962 Italian Grand Prix at Monza. From left, Roy Salvadori, John Surtees, Count Carel Godin de Beaufort, Tony Maggs, Innes Ireland (with inevitable cigarette), Graham Hill and Jimmy Clark, wearing protection from flying stones.

pp. 6/7 The Reims straight stretches ahead as the 1958 French Grand Prix is about to start. Mike Hawthorn's Ferrari won from Stirling Moss' Vanwall, but down at the back is Cliff Allison's Lotus 12, which lasted six laps. Graham Hill's Lotus 16 is on his left and American visitor Troy Ruttman, whose Scuderia Centro-Sud Maserati 250F finished 10th, on his right.

pp. 8/9 Today's master on his way to his first World Championship title. Michael Schumacher hustles the Benetton-Ford B194 towards his eighth victory of the season in the 1994 European Grand Prix at Jerez. Three weeks later Damon Hill beat him in the rain in Japan, but in the final round in Australia the rivals collided into retirement, and Schumacher was Champion by one point.

pp. 14/15 Tazio Nuvolari wipes his goggles as he storms through the village of Gueux in his 2.6 Alfa Romeo P3 during the 1932 French Grand Prix at Reims. Under a blazing sun, Nuvolari averaged 92.2 mph for the entire five-hour race, with a fastest lap at 99.5 mph, leading home his Scuderia Ferrari team-mates Borzacchini and Caracciola in an Alfa 1-2-3.

pp. 22/23 Ferrari team-mates: Juan Manuel Fangio leads Eugenio Castellotti and eventual winner Peter Collins out of the Thillois Hairpin at Reims during the 1956 French Grand Prix. The cars are Ferrari-Lancias, modified versions of the D50s taken over from the defunct Lancia team and with their pannier fuel tanks now faired into the main bodywork.

pp. 30/31 At Monaco in 1956, Fangio prepares for some practice laps in a Lancia-Ferrari D50 V8. During the race he stopped with clutch problems, took over team-mate Peter Collins' car and fought back to second place, finishing 6 secs behind Stirling Moss' Maserati. Two of the five D50s Ferrari took to Monaco still carried their pannier tanks separately mounted: the others were now faired in.

pp. 42/43 Stirling Moss always preferred to drive British cars, and had one of his finest F1 seasons in 1958 for Vanwall. He won three of the nine Grands Prix he started in the distinctive high-tailed cars, and was leading three more when the car let him down. He missed being World Champion by one point to Hawthorn, who only won one race in the more reliable Ferrari. But Vanwall were Constructors' Champions in this, the first year of that contest.

pp. 56/57 The monocoque Lotus 25, with its reclining driving position and slender cockpit giving minimal frontal area, was a classic Chapman design, and Jim Clark exploited it to the full. Here Jimmy swings through Thillois Hairpin at Reims during the 1963 French Grand Prix on his way to scoring a copybook Clark victory: he qualified on pole, led from start to finish, set fastest lap, and was more than a minute ahead of the pursuit at the chequered flag.

pp. 66/67 Airborne at Ballaugh Bridge. In the 1959 Isle of Man Senior TT John Surtees had a legendary ride on the glorious MV four. From a standing start he broke the great Bob McIntyre's Gilera lap record and then, in appalling weather, went on to win by an incredible 4m 23s. When I interviewed him, wet and chilled to the bone, he could hardly speak.

pp. 94/95 James Hunt lucked into the McLaren team in 1976 when Fittipaldi left, and crashed in his first race. But from then on he drove the season of his life. He scored seven victories (including the disallowed British GP win), and his last-gasp third place in the rain in Japan was enough to beat Lauda to the title by a single point.

pp. 110/111 Nigel Mansell spent two years at Ferrari, happily leading the team in 1989 and then less happily feeling under Prost's shadow in 1990. However in his last race for the Scuderia, the Australian Grand Prix, he had a tremendous battle for the lead with Senna's McLaren before sliding down an escape road. Senna later hit the barriers, while Mansell recovered to finish second to Piquet's Benetton.

pp. 124/125 Martin Brundle's final Formula One year was with Jordan in 1996, when Eddie's team was using the V10 Peugeot engine. It was a tough year for Martin, and he retired in half the season's rounds. But when he finished he was usually in the points: at Monza he was fourth, and at Suzuda, his 158th and final Grand Prix, he was fifth.

pp. 132/133 When conditions were difficult, Ayrton Senna's racing genius always came to the fore. In the 1993 European Grand Prix at Donington, track conditions were constantly changing, from damp and slippery to torrentially wet. It was one of those races where one man stood out head and shoulders above everybody else. On the opening lap he went from fifth place to first, and stayed there.

pp. 146/147 Michael Schumacher is without dispute today's top Formula One driver. Here he rides a Monte Carlo kerb in the 2000 Monaco Grand Prix. Comfortably in the lead, he was robbed of a fifth win around the Principality by an unusual Ferrari failure: a broken exhaust roasted a rear suspension arm until it broke.

pp. 148/149 Pitstops are an integral part of modern Formula One racing, and the pit crew carry a huge responsibility for their drivers' race positions. With three men per wheel, two on the jacks, the refuelling crew, the visor cleaner and the lollipop man, up to 20 people are involved in six frenetic seconds of activity. This Ferrari stop is in the 1999 San Marino Grand Prix, which Michael Schumacher won.

Far left: **pp. 172/173** Logistically Formula One today is an operation of immense proportions, involving each team taking tons of equipment to 17 races in 15 countries across five continents in 33 weeks. For the European races most of the kit travels by road in fleets of giant transporters which are then lined up in the paddock with geometrical precision, exactly as prescribed by Bernie Ecclestone.
This is the Imola paddock before the 2000 San Marino Grand Prix.

Left: **pp. 182/183** Monaco, 1999. Eddie Irvine hustles his Ferrari 399 up the hill from St Devote to Casino Square on his way to an inspired 2nd place behind his team-mate Michael Schumacher.

PICTURE CREDITS